Union Pu

The Colorado River

By Dale-Marie Bryan

Subject Consultant
Joseph J. Kerski, Geographer
U.S. Geological Survey
Denver, Colorado

Reading Consultant
Cecilia Minden-Cupp, PhD
Former Director of the Language and Literacy Program
Harvard Graduate School of Education
Cambridge, Massachusetts

Children's Press®
A Division of Scholastic Inc.
New York   Toronto   London   Auckland   Sydney
Mexico City   New Delhi   Hong Kong
Danbury, Connecticut

Designer: Herman Adler Design
Photo Researcher: Caroline Anderson
The photo on the cover shows the Colorado River near Moab, Utah.

Library of Congress Cataloging-in-Publication Data

Bryan, Dale-Marie, 1953–
    The Colorado River / by Dale-Marie Bryan ; subject consultant,
Joseph J. Kerski ; reading consultant, Cecilia Minden-Cupp.
        p. cm. — (Rookie Read-About Geography)
    Includes index.
    ISBN 0-516-25033-7 (lib. bdg.)   0-516-21447-0 (pbk.)
    1. Colorado River (Colo.—Mexico)—Juvenile literature. 2. Colorado
River (Colo.—Mexico)—Geography—Juvenile literature. I. Title.
II. Series.
    F788.B76 2006
    917.91'3   2005021748

JE
BRY
c. 1

7/06

CHILDREN'S PRESS, and ROOKIE READ-ABOUT®,
and associated logos are trademarks and/or registered trademarks
of Scholastic Library Publishing. SCHOLASTIC and associated logos
are trademarks and/or registered trademarks of Scholastic Inc.

1 2 3 4 5 6 7 8 9 10 R 15 14 13 12 11 10 09 08 07 06

The Colorado River has
many important jobs.

The river flows through dams to make electricity. It brings drinking water to cities. It irrigates, or waters, crops.

This irrigation system is connected to the Colorado River.

The Colorado River begins as melting snow. It flows from the Rocky Mountains through canyons and deserts. It moves fast in certain places. The fast parts are called rapids.

Colorado is Spanish for "colored red." Early Spanish explorers thought the river looked red.

Silt causes this coloring. Silt is a mixture of tiny pieces of sand, clay, and rock.

The Green River joining the Colorado River

The Colorado River is the seventh-longest river in the United States. Other rivers flow into it, including the Green River and the San Juan River.

The Colorado River used to empty into the Gulf of California. But many people use the Colorado River. Now it usually dries up before reaching the ocean.

The Gulf of California

The Colorado River carved the Grand Canyon. Rain and blowing sand made the canyon bigger.

The Grand Canyon is one of the largest canyons in the world.

John Wesley Powell was a geologist in the 1800s. A geologist is someone who studies rocks.

Powell led boat trips through the Grand Canyon. He was the first person to create a map of the Colorado River.

17

Hoover Dam

18

The Colorado River
once flooded in spring.
In summer, it nearly dried
up. People built dams to
control the river. Dams
also store river water.

Hoover Dam is the biggest
dam on the Colorado
River. It is on the border
of Arizona and Nevada.

Droughts have also changed the flow of the Colorado River. A drought is a period of dryness when there is little rain or snow.

Droughts are harmful to local wildlife. Many plants and animals depend on the Colorado River to survive.

The Colorado River during a drought

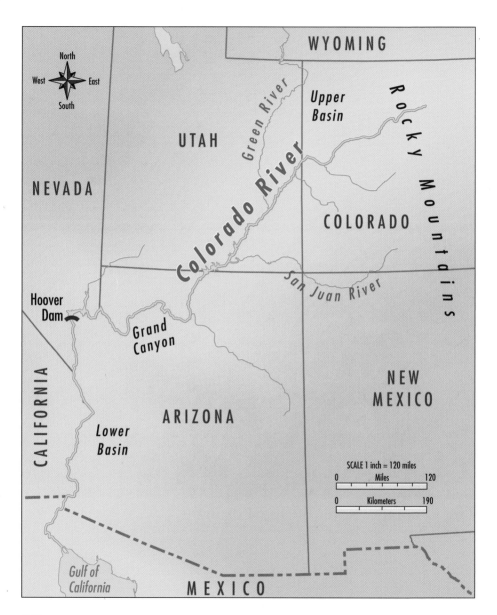

North
West ✦ East
South

WYOMING

Green River

Upper
Basin

UTAH

NEVADA

Colorado River

ROCKY

COLORADO

Mountains

San Juan River

Hoover
Dam

Grand
Canyon

NEW
MEXICO

CALIFORNIA

Lower
Basin

ARIZONA

SCALE 1 inch = 120 miles

0	Miles	120

0	Kilometers	190

Gulf of
California

MEXICO

The Colorado River is called the Lifeline of the Southwest. A lifeline is something that saves or protects people. Seven states depend on the Colorado River for water. These are Wyoming, Colorado, Utah, Nevada, Arizona, California, and New Mexico. Mexico also depends on the Colorado River.

The states once argued
over who had rights to the
Colorado River. In 1922,
the states agreed to share
rights to the river water.

They divided the Colorado
River basin into two
sections. These became the
Upper and Lower basins.
A basin is an area of land
that is drained by a river.

The Upper Basin

The Lower Basin

Bighorn sheep

Evergreen forests grow in the Upper Basin. Bighorn sheep and elk live there.

The Lower Basin is home to coyotes and prairie dogs. Sagebrush and small pines grow in this area.

Prairie dog

People raft and tube
on the Colorado River.
They fish and camp along
its banks.

What would you like to
do on the Colorado River?

Rafting on the Colorado River

Words You Know

bighorn sheep

Grand Canyon

Hoover Dam

prairie dog

rapids

Rocky Mountains

Index

About the Author

This is Dale-Marie Bryan's second book for children. When she isn't writing, she enjoys reading and helping her husband on their farm in western Kansas.

Photo Credits

Photographs © 2006: Alamy Images: 9 (Richard Levine), 14, 30 bottom (Barrie Rokeach); Corbis Images: 6, 31 bottom right (Jose Fuste Raga/zefa), 18, 31 top left (Lester Lefkowitz), 25 top (Danny Lehman), 13 (Neil Rabinowitz), 29, 31 bottom left (Scott T. Smith), 17; Dembinsky Photo Assoc./Dan Dempster: cover; Getty Images/David McNew: 21; Lonely Planet Images/Jim Wark: 10; Masterfile/Ron Stroud: 3; Peter Arnold Inc./Matt Meadows: 5; Photo Researchers, NY: 27, 31 top right (G. C. Kelley), 26, 30 top (Craig K. Lorenz); Superstock, Inc./Wilburn D. Murphy: 25 bottom.

Map by Bob Italiano